W9-BQZ-731

IN A SACRED MANNER WE LIVE

Introduction & Commentary by Don D. Fowler

Selection of Photography by Rachel J. Homer

Millis Public Library
Auburn Road
Millis, Mass. 02054

IN A SACRED MANNER WE LIVE

Photographs of

the North American Indian by

EDWARD S. CURTIS

WEATHERVANE BOOKS • NEW YORK

45245

DEC. 10 1991

970.1
CURT

COPYRIGHT © MCMLXXII BY BARRE PUBLISHERS
LIBRARY OF CONGRESS CATALOG CARD NUMBER: 73-185614
ALL RIGHTS RESERVED.
THIS EDITION IS PUBLISHED BY WEATHERVANE BOOKS
A DIVISION OF IMPRINT SOCIETY, INC., DISTRIBUTED BY CROWN PUBLISHERS, INC.
f g h

TABLE OF CONTENTS

IN A SACRED MANNER WE LIVE has been designed by David Godine. The Frontispiece and photographs on pages 23, 26, 27, 36–38, 40, 46, 56–59, 63, 66, 67, 71–73, 85, 90, 103, 115, 123, 135, and 138 have been printed from negatives belonging to The Pierpont Morgan Library's Curtis collection and are reproduced with the Library's permission. The remainder of the photographs have been printed from original plates in the Boston Public Library's set of Edward S. Curtis's THE NORTH AMERICAN INDIAN, with the kind cooperation of John Alden, Keeper of Rare Books.

IN A SACRED
MANNER WE LIVE

EDWARD S. CURTIS

EDWARD S. CURTIS devoted twenty-five years of his life to the development of a photographic and ethnographic record of the Indian peoples of western North America. The results of this devotion are embodied in his twenty-volume magnum opus, *The North American Indian*. The photographs presented in these volumes are truly works of art. However, the original limited edition of 500 sets has made his art relatively inaccessible. The present volume makes available a selection of his photographs to a broader public.

Although he worked in the early years of the present century, Curtis may be said to be the last of the great 19th-century photographers of Western America—for he was documenting ways of life which were in full flower during the 1800's but by 1900 had been trampled by America's rush west to fulfill its self-proclaimed Manifest Destiny. At the turn of the 20th century, western American Indians were on reservations and the old ways were but memories in the minds of aging men.

The war over territory had been won by the whites. The last semblance of Indian armed resistance ebbed away in the blood of those massacred at Wounded Knee in 1890. Now there was a war for the minds of those Indians still remaining. In the 1870's General William Tecumseh Sherman had declared that "the only good Indian is a dead Indian." In 1900, missionaries and Indian agents were saying that "the only good Indian is a Christian farmer in overalls." The Indians' nomadic life and "pagan" ceremonies and beliefs were to be stamped out at all costs.

In Curtis's eyes, and those of others, "the Indian" was doomed inevitably to vanish, if not physically at least culturally. Such a fate had been predicted by others for over a century, from Thomas Jefferson in the 1780's to John Wesley Powell in the 1870's. Throughout the 19th century, scholars such as Lewis Cass, Henry Rowe Schoolcraft, Lewis Henry Morgan, George Bird Grinnell and John Wesley Powell and many others bent their efforts to "salvage, for posterity," what knowledge they could about the history, languages and cultures of the "Vanishing Savages."

By 1900 anthropologists from the Bureau of Ethnology of the Smithsonian Institution and from several universities were in the field recording the old Indian ways, "before it's too late." There was also a nostalgic and romantic interest on the part of a public fascinated by the West and the Indians in it. Edward S. Curtis like many others became caught up in this fascination—and he was determined to join in the effort to put on record knowledge of the Indians and their past ways of life. He devoted twenty-five years to the task and completed it through a combination of luck, circumstance and dogged, painstaking work.

Edward S. Curtis was born in 1868 near Whitewater, Wisconsin, the second of four children born to Johnson and Ella Sheriff Curtis. Early in his life, he became fascinated with photography, and as a young man he built a camera and later worked as a darkroom assistant in Saint Paul, Minnesota.

In 1887 the Curtis family moved to Seattle, Washington. The father died soon thereafter and Edward and the family were hard pressed to make ends meet. Edward spent as much time as possible in making photographs. He soon became interested in the Indians around Puget Sound, began photographing them, and sold prints through a local dealer. In 1892 Curtis married Clara Phillips and acquired his own photographic studio. He continued to photograph Indians and some of his prints won prizes in local and national shows.

The turning point in Curtis's life came in 1898. He was climbing on Mount Rainier to make some photographs when he came upon a party of lost climbers. He guided them back to camp. The party included C. Hart Merriam, then Chief of the United States Biological Survey, and George Bird Grinnell, editor of *Field and Stream* magazine and a famed student of Plains Indians.

Curtis, Grinnell and Merriam became close friends. The following year Merriam arranged for Curtis to become the photographer for the Harriman Expedition to Alaska. The expedition was headed and financed by Edward H. Harriman, the railroad tycoon. Initially planned as a pleasure cruise for the Harriman family, the trip was expanded to a full-fledged scientific expedition to study the Alaska Coast. The twenty-five man scientific staff included Grinnell and Merriam and, among others, Frederick V. Colville, Curator of the National Herbarium of the U.S. Department of Agriculture; William Healey Dall, of the U.S. Geological Survey and an expert on Alaskan geology and anthropology; Daniel Elliott, Curator of the Field Columbian Museum in Chicago; Grove Karl Gilbert, of the U.S. Geological Survey; and John Muir, listed in the expedition reports as "Author and Student of Glaciers," but now renowned as a conservationist and founder of the Sierra Club. One of the artists accompanying the expedition was Frederick S. Dellenbaugh, who had accompanied John Wesley Powell on the second expedition down the Colorado River in 1871–72 and achieved later fame as an artist, author and explorer.

The expedition spent the months of June and July, 1899, coasting the shores of Alaska, studying the mountains, glaciers, flora and fauna and the Indians. Curtis and his assistant, D. G. Inverarity, took several thousand photographs. Ultimately, under the editorship of Merriam, fourteen large volumes were published by the Smithsonian Institution reporting the scientific results of the expedition. Curtis's photographs were used as illustrations in several of the volumes.

In 1900 Grinnell invited Curtis to accompany him on a visit to the Blackfeet Indians of Montana. Grinnell was an honorary chief of the tribe and well respected by them. He and Curtis spent the summer on the reservation. During this time Curtis apparently resolved to embark on a project of photographing and studying all the Indians west of the Mississippi River. Grinnell encouraged him, although they both realized the vastness of the project.

Curtis returned to Seattle, arranged his business affairs and set out for Arizona. He had little money, but high hopes and a sense of purpose. He planned to finance his work through the sale of prints and the profits from his studio, which was now a family enterprise.

Curtis traveled first to the Pueblos of Arizona and New Mexico, the Hopi, Zuni, Acoma and the Pueblos of the Upper Rio Grande Valley. He then moved to the Colorado River tribes, the Mohave, Maricopa and Yuma, then to the Pima and Papago of the Arizona Sonoran desert. From there he moved to the various Apache groups in Arizona and New Mexico and to the Apache's close linguistic relatives, the Navajo. He next visited the Yavapai, Walapai and Havasupai along the south rim of the Grand Canyon. In the following years he visited many of the tribes of the Great Plains, the Sioux, Cheyenne, Crow, Blackfeet and others, and the Nez Percé and other tribes of the Rocky Mountains.

In 1904 Curtis returned to Seattle with over one thousand negatives. He began to sell some prints and put on an exhibition at a local hall. The exhibit was a signal success. In 1905, with the aid of E. H. Harriman and Curtis's Washington friends from the Alaska Expedition, Curtis's work was exhibited in Washington at the Washington Club, the Cosmos Club and an art gallery. Curtis was invited to photograph a group of visiting Indians on the White House lawn. The group included the famed Apache Chief Geronimo, whom Curtis knew, and together they were introduced to President Theodore Roosevelt. Through the Harriman family, arrangements were made for Curtis's exhibit to move to the Waldorf-Astoria in New York. It was a great success. Many of his prints were purchased by prominent members of New York society.

In 1905 Grinnell published an article in *Scribner's Magazine* calling attention to Curtis's work, and illustrated it with thirteen of his photographs. The following year Curtis himself was invited to publish articles in *Scribner's,* which he did, illustrating them with additional photographs.

In 1905–06 Curtis again returned to the East Coast. He gave illustrated lectures in Washington to audiences of over one thousand. He received acclaim for his exhibit of photographs in Boston, Pittsburgh and for a second exhibit at the Waldorf in New York.

In early 1906, Theodore Roosevelt called Curtis to the White House to discuss his work. Roosevelt was obviously pleased with Curtis's project and recognized the need for adequate financing. He suggested that Curtis seek help from J. Pierpont Morgan. An appointment was arranged. Morgan looked through Curtis's portfolio—and agreed to support the work in the amount of $75,000, stipulating that he wanted to see the photographs incorporated in a set of books, "the handsomest ever published." Curtis's work was now assured, and he set out to collect the data and make the pictures. He was temporarily diverted for some weeks taking portraits of the Roosevelt children, and later acted as official photographer for the wedding of Alice Roosevelt and Nicholas Longworth.

But from 1906 through 1927 Curtis and his assistants, especially W. E. Myers, spent most of each year traveling from reservation to reservation, learning all they could about the old ways of Indian life, their subsistence, arts, marriage, family life, political organization, myths and tales, history and biography of prominent men—and making more photographs.

Curtis was very interested in the history of Indian-White relations, as seen from the Indians' standpoint. Together with three Crow Indian scouts who had served with Custer, Curtis toured the battlefield on the Little Big Horn. The scouts had been sent away just before the final stand by one of Custer's aides, who told them, "You have done what you have agreed to do—brought us to the Sioux camp; now go back to the pack train and live."[1] From Red Cloud, the well-known Oglala Sioux chief who led his men in the famed Wagon Box fight in 1867 against the U.S. Army, Curtis learned and reported the Indians' side of events in the Dakotas from 1866 to 1876 which led to the Custer massacre. He talked with Chief Joseph, leader of the Nez Percé, who so valiantly resisted White encroachment and were finally pursued into Canada and "pacified." Chief Joseph vowed, then, that he would "fight no more, forever."

The first of the planned twenty volumes appeared in 1907. This and subsequent volumes were edited by Frederick Webb Hodge, of the Bureau of American Ethnology who, at the time, was finishing the editing of another monumental study of American Indians, the encyclopedic two-volume *Handbook of American Indians North of Mexico*, a project begun nearly forty years earlier by John Wesley Powell, the founder of the Bureau.

The full title page of volume I tells Curtis's story:

THE NORTH AMERICAN INDIAN

Being a Series of Volumes Picturing and Describing the Indians of the United States and Alaska, written, illustrated and published by Edward S. Curtis, edited by Frederick Webb Hodge, foreword by Theodore Roosevelt, field research conducted under the patronage of J. Pierpont Morgan, in twenty volumes.

In the *General Introduction* Curtis noted that his work "represents the result of a personal study of a people who are rapidly losing the traces of the aboriginal character and who are destined ultimately to become assimilated with the 'superior race.'"[2] He went on to say, "It has been the aim to picture all features of the Indian life and environment—types of the young and old, with their habitations, industries, ceremonies, games and everyday customs."[3]

Curtis did not totally fulfill his aim. He dealt, first of all, only with Western Indians, those who lived aboriginally west of the Mississippi, or who were moved to Indian Territory during the 19th century. Further, his coverage of some areas and tribes was superficial because the tribes were extinct or nearly so, or, in some cases, work by contemporaries, such as A. L. Kroeber, Clark Wissler and George Bird Grinnell, rendered his efforts redundant. In some few cases he was able to add little that was new; in others he made signal contributions to ethnography. But his hauntingly beautiful photographs were, in all cases, valuable ethnographically as well as artistically.

Curtis encountered many difficulties in his work. The sheer logistical task of traveling by wagon or pack horse to the many reservations was made doubly difficult by the heavy large-format camera equipment of the time. But even more difficult was the task faced by every anthropologist, that of gaining rapport with peoples made hostile by a hundred years of adverse relations with Whites. Inquiry into the esoterica of native myth, religion and ritual was especially difficult. Such matters were not for uninitiated outsiders. As Curtis wrote, "The task has not been an easy one . . .

it . . . often required days and weeks of patient endeavor before my assistants and I succeeded in overcoming the deep-rooted superstition, conservatism, and secretiveness so characteristic of primitive people, who are ever loath to afford a glimpse of their inner life to those who are not of their own. . . ."[4]

But Curtis persevered, spurred on by his felt need to record as much as possible before the knowledge was lost forever: "The passing of every old man or woman means the passing of some tradition, some knowledge of sacred rites possessed by no other; consequently the information that is to be gathered, for the benefit of future generations, respecting the mode of life of one of the great races of mankind, must be collected at once or the opportunity will be lost for all time."[5]

Curtis did not collect a "complete" ethnography on any one tribe—to do so would have taken many lifetimes. In fact, despite the work of Curtis and hundreds of others, the available information on many tribes is scant even yet. But for some tribes, Curtis's data are very valuable, especially the Hopi and Navajo of Arizona, some of the Plains tribes and the Kwakiutl of the Northwest Coast.

Although Curtis was obviously enamoured of "the Indian" and came increasingly to sympathize with their plight and be angered by the injustices done them, he nevertheless liked some groups better than others. This liking seemed to be determined by personalities, and perhaps implicitly, by how closely various tribes appeared to him to fit a Horatio Alger image of industriousness and forthrightness. Thus he wrote, "the Hopi are without doubt among the most interesting of our surviving American Indians."[6] Although he spent parts of four field seasons with the Kwakiutl and devoted an entire volume to them, he was not impressed by their personalities: "It is scarcely an exaggeration to say that no single noble trait redeems the Kwakiutl character."[7] He was impressed by the physiques and physical prowess of the Mohave of the Lower Colorado River, but wrote, "Mentally, they are dull and slow—brothers to the ox."[8] Later studies, notably those by A. L. Kroeber, found the mental life of the Mohave exceedingly rich and varied.

The last volume of Curtis's great work appeared in 1930. Fittingly, the volume was on the Eskimo whom he had first seen in 1898 as a member of the Harriman Expedition. He was very impressed by the Eskimo and his way of life so closely adapted to a harsh environment. The Eskimo people, he wrote, "are healthy, as a rule, and exceptionally happy because they have been little affected by contact with civilization."[9]

Curtis's *The North American Indian* can only be described as monumental. The twenty large volumes, each nearly 300 pages in length, and the accompanying twenty folios contain over 2,200 photographs, each a masterpiece of the photographer's art. Additionally, the several thousand pages of text contain a plentitude of information of great value to anthropologists, historians, linguists and ethnomusicologists.

With the publication of Volume xx, Edward Curtis's task was finished. He continued to lead an active life, pursuing mining interests and work as a photographer until his death in Los Angeles in 1952. He had built his own monument, a unique legacy of scholarship and artistry which serves as a poignant reminder to all who see his work of the rich ways of life lived by the first inhabitants of the New World — the American Indian.

Perhaps the most fitting tribute to Curtis's work was written by George Bird Grinnell. Although written in 1905, the tribute could equally well describe the completed work in 1930: "I speak of Curtis's work as photography and of his pictures as photographs; but these terms are misleading to anyone who, in thinking of a photograph, forms a mental picture only of the photographs that he has seen. The results which Curtis gets with his camera stir one as one is stirred by a great painting; and when we are thus moved by a picture, and share the thought and feeling that the artist had when he made the picture, we may recognize it as a work of art."[10]

THE INDIANS

AT THE TIME of European discovery of the North American continent, it was occupied by several million people who came to be called Indians. These people spoke several hundred different languages which anthropologists were later to classify into some fifty-eight language families. The cultures of the Indians were equally various, usually closely adapted to the different ecological areas in which they lived—the eastern forests, the Plains, the mountains and deserts of the Great Basin and the Southwest, the forests of the Northwest Coast.

The Indians of what is now the United States and Canada had not developed the high civilizations characteristic of Meso- and South American areas, although there had been great ceremonial centers in the Mississippi and Ohio Valleys and the Southeast in past millennia. The North American Indians had, however, been influenced by the developments in Meso-America—receiving domesticated plants, possibly pottery, and a variety of ceremonial features from that area.

Early European influence impinged on the Indians from the Eastern Seaboard and from the South through Mexico. The impact was dramatic, and usually disastrous for the Indians. The Spanish *Entrada* into the Southwest, beginning in 1540 with Coronado's abortive search for the fabled golden cities of Cibola, and the firm establishment of Spanish rule in the 1600's, had a profound effect on the Puebloan and other peoples living in what is now Arizona, New Mexico and western Texas. Indirectly, there was also an effect on the tribes of the Rocky Mountains and the High Plains through the spread of horses to tribes in those areas after A.D. 1680. One result of the spread of horses was the conversion of many semi-sedentary earth-lodge-dwelling farmers along the rivers of the High Plains into nomadic buffalo hunters. Many inhabitants of the northern and central Rockies and the adjacent High Plains were well equipped with horses and sometimes guns, long before they had any systematic contact with Whites. Lewis and Clark in 1803–05 found Indians all the way to the Pacific Ocean equipped with horses. Therefore, by 1800 Indian culture in North America had in some areas been drastically changed by the animals and firearms introduced by Whites—although only east of the Mississippi and in the Southwest were various Indians in direct and continued contact with Whites prior to that time.

The westward expansion of Whites changed all this. Between 1800 and 1890 the inexorable westward movement and "civilizing" of the trans-Mississippi area and the Far West by Whites changed Indian life completely. Every tribe was affected. Populations declined drastically from warfare and introduced diseases. By 1890 the numerous and varied "independent nations" of Indians were no more. The survivors had become "wards of the government," herded onto reservations, small islands in a sea of alien culture. Only in limited areas, such as the Southwest, were Indians able to retain some measure of their cultural integrity and political independence.

It was against this historical background that Edward Curtis began his work. Curtis wrote about and photographed the majority of the tribes of the western United States, as well as a few Canadian tribes and some of the Eskimo groups along part of the Alaskan Coast. He devoted some volumes to specific tribes. Other volumes contain descriptions of a group of tribes within one area. Curtis also devoted part of one volume to the Indians of Oklahoma, discussing briefly tribes or remnant tribes moved from east of the Mississippi to Indian Territory during the 19th century. But his major focus was on tribes whose homelands in early historic times were west of the Mississippi. The Indians in Curtis's photographs can be grouped into several geographical areas: the Southwest, the Plains, the Plateau, the Northwest Coast, the Desert West, northern and central California and the Eskimos of the western coast of Alaska.

FOG-IN-THE-MORNING (APSAROKE)

THE PLAINS

THE HIGH PLAINS include the area of North America between the Rocky Mountains and the 100th western meridian from southern Alberta to Texas. The area was occupied by a diverse number of tribes in historical times. Prior to the advent of horses, many of the tribes were earth-lodge-dwelling farmers, living along the Missouri and its tributaries and other eastward-flowing streams. Others, notably the Dakota or "Sioux" tribes, lived in the prairie region of present-day Minnesota and northern Iowa. The more northerly groups, such as the Cree and Chipewyan, originally came from the lake and forest regions of south-central Canada. The Comanche, who dominated the Llano Estacado of New Mexico and west Texas were originally from the Great Basin. By about A.D. 1500 they had moved onto the plains of southeastern Wyoming, and then pushed southward after the advent of horses.

Once horses reached the northern Plains, several groups including the Chipewyan, Arapaho, Cree, Atsina, Piegan, Blackfeet, Blood, Cheyenne, the several Sioux or Dakota tribes, the Assiniboin and Crow abandoned their earth lodges and farm plots to become full time buffalo hunters, living in skin tipis and developing military societies and a highly structured system of warfare.

Some tribes, especially the Arikara, Mandan and Hidatsa, although adopting horses, remained as earth-lodge dwellers along the Middle Missouri. These tribes became middlemen between other Indians and fur traders in the early part of the 19th century.

Curtis spent several seasons among the Plains Indians. Of them he wrote, "In gathering the lore of the Indians of the Plains one hears only of yesterday. His [sic] thoughts are of the past; today is but a living death, and his very being is permeated with the hopelessness of tomorrow." [11]

By Curtis's day the buffalo were gone—and with them the mainstay of Plains Indian life. The Plains Indian had developed the art of warfare and raiding to a high degree. For years the Comanche held the Whites at bay, until overwhelmed by the superior fire power of repeating arms. The northern Plains tribes defended their homelands for nearly 70 years—alternately ceding portions to the govern-

[19]

ment and then having to fight encroachments on the lands set aside for them. They won at Little Big Horn in 1876, but were finally defeated, the last resistance coming at Wounded Knee in 1890. When Curtis began his work among the Plains tribes in 1905, they possessed the regalia, and the memories of war, valor and counting of coups. But, like the buffalo, it was all in the past: "one hears only of yesterday." Ceremonialism continued in the Sun Dance, which Curtis photographed among the Northern Cheyenne and in the newly emerging Peyote Cult. Many of the Indians were still living in tipis, but they were more often made of canvas supplied by the government than of elk or buffalo hides.

Curtis spent parts of 1905, 1907 and 1908 studying several of the Northern Plains tribes. As noted in the introduction, he toured the Custer battlefield with Custer's Crow scouts, and wrote a long essay on details of the battle as seen by the Indians. He later moved to the Dakotas to study the remnants of the Arikara, Mandan and Hidatsa tribes—the earth-lodge dwellers of the Middle Missouri who had figured so prominently in the early days of the fur trade. He chronicled the decline of these tribes—decimated as they were by smallpox, liquor and warfare. They retained some vestiges of their old ceremonial cycle—and Curtis was able to convince them to reenact parts of some ceremonies for him. Many of the men retained their ceremonial regalia and Curtis photographed them in it, such as Bear's Belly, an Arikara man, shown wrapped in his sacred bear skin.

In later years, Curtis expanded his investigations of Northern Plains tribes to include the Chipewyan, the Western Woods Cree and the Sarsi of Canada. Much of this work was devoted to ritual and ceremonial, including practices centering on capturing eagles and placating the Eagle Spirit.

Finally, Curtis journeyed to Oklahoma to study the Comanche, Wichita, Southern Cheyenne and Southern Arapaho who lived on reservations there. He also briefly described the many other Indians of Oklahoma who had been removed to Indian Territory from east of the Mississippi during the 19th century. His many photographs of the Plains tribes capture, succinctly, the glories of the past. But in the eyes of the men and women who posed for him one can also read the sadness of the "living death" of the present.

CUSTER'S CROW SCOUTS

DAUGHTER OF AMERICAN HORSE (TETON SIOUX)

LITTLE HAWK, BRULE (TETON SIOUX)

MOTHER AND CHILD (TETON SIOUX)

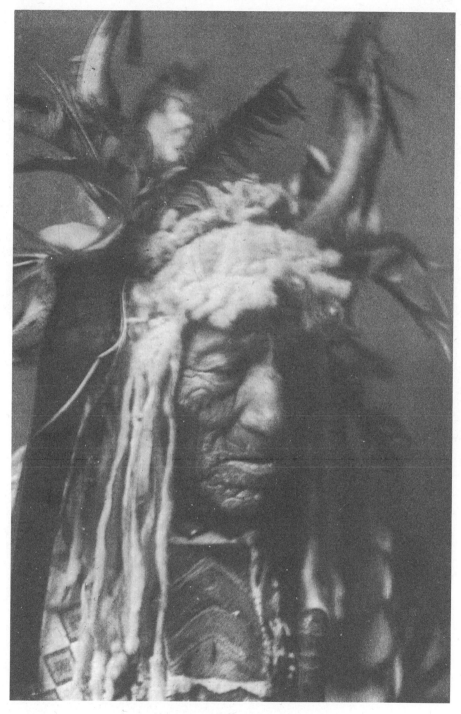

LEAN WOLF (HIDATSA)

TWO PIEGAN

[26]

IN BLACK CANYON (APSAROKE)

SHOT-IN-THE-HAND (APSAROKE)

MANDAN BUFFALO BERRY GATHERERS

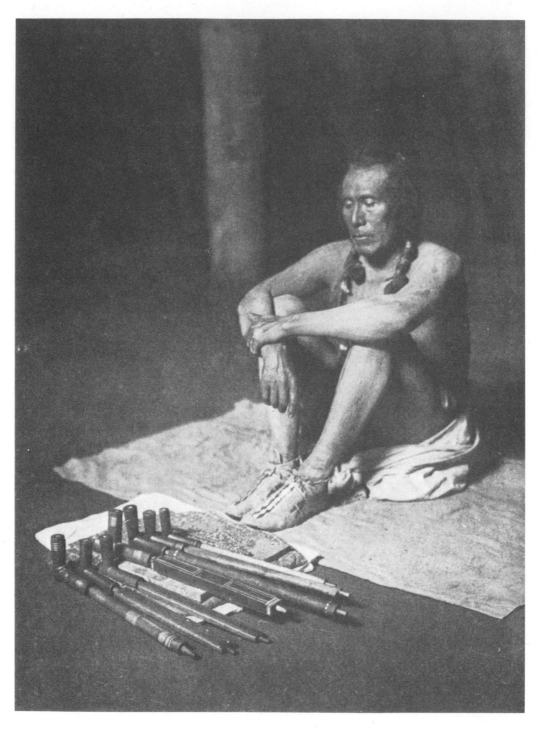

IN THE ARIKARA MEDICINE LODGE

ATSINA CRAZY DANCERS

BEAR'S BELLY (ARIKARA)

A PIEGAN HOME

CHEYENNE SUN DANCE IN PROGRESS

THE PIEGAN

[35]

PASSING THE CLIFFS (APSAROKE)

PORCUPINE (CHEYENNE)

CHEYENNE WAITING IN THE FOREST

CHIPEWYAN BERRY PICKERS IN CAMP

ASSINIBOIN PLACATING THE SPIRIT OF A SLAIN EAGLE

A BLOOD HORSEMAN

CREE TIPIS

WOLF-CHILD (BLOOD)

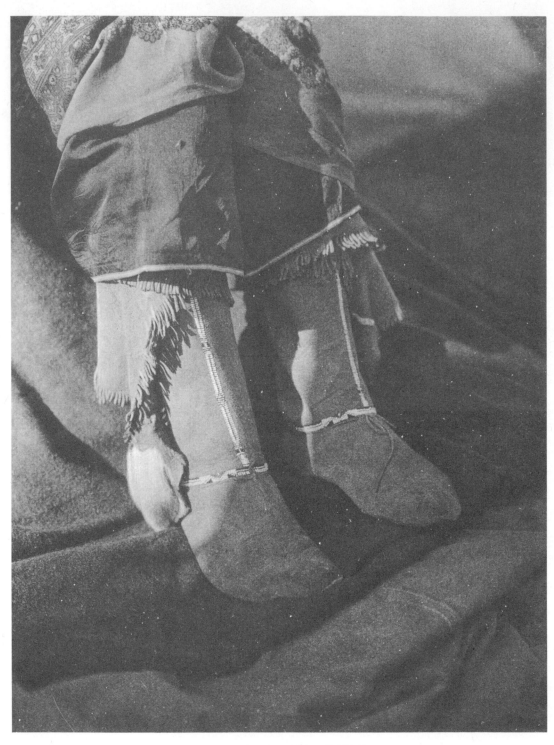

COMANCHE FOOTWEAR

COMANCHE MOTHERS

SACRED BAGS OF THE HORN SOCIETY (BLOOD)

BUFFALO

OLD ARAPAHO WARRIOR

FRAME OF A PEYOTE SWEAT LODGE

WICHITA GRASS HOUSE

ANIMAL DANCE AT THE POOL (CHEYENNE)

THE SOUTHWEST

THE SOUTHWEST, including the present states of Arizona and New Mexico and parts of west Texas and northern Mexico, was occupied by numerous tribes which can be grouped into five divisions: the Pueblos, the Navajos and Apaches, the Pimans and Maricopas of south-central Arizona, the Upland Yumans of western and northwestern Arizona, and the River Yumans along the lower Colorado River.

The Pueblo tribes are usually divided into eastern and western groups. The eastern group includes the several villages along the Rio Grande Valley in New Mexico, from Taos in the north to Isleta in the south, including Tesuque, Pojoaque, Nambe, San Ildefonso, Santa Clara, San Juan, Picuris, Sandia, Santo Domingo, Zia, San Felipe and Cochiti. The western group includes the Hopi villages of Arizona, and Zuni, Acoma and Laguna of western New Mexico. The Eastern and Western Pueblos are alike in being farmers, living in compact adobe villages, and having generally similar political and ceremonial organizations, beliefs and rituals, especially with regard to weather control, fertility and harmony with the universe. They differ, however, in kinship, some social practices and ceremonial details. The Pueblos have been more successful than many other American Indians in maintaining their cultural integrity, despite nearly 300 years of Spanish domination and 130 years of American influence.

The Navajo and their close linguistic relatives, the Apache, were relative latecomers to the Southwest, having migrated from interior Canada in late prehistoric times. Little is known, although much is conjectured, about Navajo-Apache culture prior to the historic period. They were present in the Southwest and on the Southwestern Plains when the Spanish entered the area in 1540. Once they acquired horses, beginning about 1680, they came to dominate many areas of present-day west Texas, New Mexico, Arizona and northern Mexico. They were never conquered by the Spanish and only in the 1870's and 1880's did the U.S. Army succeed in subduing them after many bloody campaigns. In historic times, Navajo and Apache culture was an amalgam of indigenous Pueblo, Plains and Spanish cultural traits. The Navajo in particular adopted many Spanish elements, including the horse, silverworking and sheep herding. Pueblo elements adopted by the Navajo include weaving, horticulture, some ceremonial beliefs and practices and possibly ways of reckoning kinship. But all these various elements were reworked into peculiarly Navajo configurations. The Apache remained more aloof from Spanish culture, but various tribes did take up farming and some were greatly influenced by Plains culture.

By the time the Southwest became United States territory in the 1840's, the Navajo were firmly established in and around the Four Corners area, the ruggedly beautiful Red Rock and Painted Desert country of Utah, Colorado, Arizona and New Mexico.

Historically, there were six major divisions or tribes of Apache. One division was the Kiowa-Apache of the Plains. They were closely associated with the Kiowa of Kansas and Oklahoma in historic times, although they retained their language, and are properly a Plains, rather than a Southwestern tribe. The Jicarilla Apache lived in northern New Mexico. They were farmers but also ranged onto the Plains to hunt buffalo. A branch of the Jicarilla, the Lipan Apache, lived in eastern New Mexico and west Texas in the early historic period but were later pushed into northern Mexico by the Comanche. The Mescalero Apache lived in south-central New Mexico and were primarily a hunting and gathering people. The Chiracahua Apache dominated southeastern Arizona but extended their range into New Mexico and northern Mexico. Like the Mescalero they were hunters and gatherers. In the late 19th century the Chiracahua were led by Cochise and Geronimo. They fiercely resisted "pacification" and were not finally subdued by the U.S. Army until the 1880's. The sixth main division of the Apache were the Western Apache of east-central Arizona, comprised of several sub-groups including the White Mountain, Cibecue, San Carlos, and Northern and Southern Tonto tribes.

The Upland Yuman group in the Southwest includes the "Pai" tribes of western and northwestern Arizona, the Walapai, Yavapai and Havasupai. Compared with the Pueblos and the Navajo and Apache peoples, these tribes had a relatively simple material, social and ritual culture. The Havasupai did some farming, especially in Cataract Canyon, a side branch of the Grand Canyon. But generally the Pai tribes were hunters and foragers. Never large in numbers, they ranged over the arid deserts and uplands of Arizona, moving through a seasonal cycle to exploit available resources.

South of the Pai tribes in central and southern Arizona were the Pima and Papago and the Yuman-speaking Maricopa. The latter were relatives of the River Yumans to the west. Most Pima and the Maricopa were farmers, practicing irrigation agriculture along the Salt and Gila rivers and living in relatively large, permanent villages. Some Pima and the Papago lived in the arid deserts south of the rivers. The lack of permanent water forced them to subsist as hunters and foragers. They lived in widely-scattered small bands, exploiting the meager resources the area provided, notably the fruit of the giant saguaro cactus.

To the west along the Lower Colorado River were the River Yumans, the Mohave, Halchidhoma, Yuma and Cocopa. These tribes farmed the rich river terraces along the Colorado River. The annual Nile-like flooding of the river terraces provided rich agricultural areas on which to grow corn, beans and squash. The people also exploited natural plants, especially the mesquite and screwbean, and obtained fish from the river. They were fierce warriors, often fighting among themselves and occasionally with the mountain and desert peoples to the east and west, although such people were not thought to be fit opponents.

Curtis visited most of the Southwestern tribes, but he was most taken with the Hopi and the Navajo. Of the latter he wrote: "The Navajo is the American Bedouin, the chief human touch in the great plateau-desert region of our Southwest, acknowledging no superior, paying allegiance to no king in name of chief, a keeper of flocks and herds who asks nothing of the Government but to be unmolested in his pastoral life and in the religion of his forebearers."[12]

Curtis was able to attend Navajo chants, or sings; nine-day ceremonies held for curing purposes and to preserve the integrity of the cosmos. He appreciated the tremendous mental effort necessary for a Navajo ceremonial leader to master a particular chant: "To completely master the intricacies of any one of the many nine days' ceremonies requires close application during the major portion of a man's lifetime."[13] But the knowledge seemed to be passing: "The medicine men recognize the fact that their ritual has been decadent for some time, and they regard it as foreordained that when all the ceremonies are forgotten the world will cease to exist."[14] Despite this pessimism, the Navajo continue to maintain their ceremonial system, though they have adapted much of the rest of their culture, as they always have in the past, to changing conditions.

Most of Curtis's work with the Apache was with the Jicarilla, but he also visited other Apache tribes and knew Geronimo, the famed Chiracahua leader. Curtis's primary achievement among the Apache was to overcome their extreme reticence to divulge anything about their ceremonial and ritual life. He was able to record a number of myths and tales and ritual details.

Curtis visited the Hopi seven times between 1900 and 1919, working principally at the village of Walpi. He was fascinated by Hopi ceremonialism, especially the Snake Dance, during which the dancers carry live rattlesnakes in their mouths during a part of the ceremony. He was able to photograph many of the preparations for the dance and the dance itself, a privilege accorded few other outsiders before or since. Curtis also made many photographs of Hopi village life, of day-to-day activities and of the Hopi girls in their traditional garb with their hair done up in large swirls, symbolic of squash blossoms and their unmarried status.

Curtis spent much less time among the other Western Pueblos and the Eastern Pueblos of New Mexico. In fact, nearly all the information on these tribes was collected by his assistants, although Curtis made the photographs. As with the Hopi, Curtis and his assistants studied and photographed aspects of daily life as well as ceremonials, but they were limited to public ceremonials, such as Catholic Feast days, and obtained very little information on indigenous ceremonies.

Curtis briefly visited the Maricopa, Pima and Papago of southern Arizona, but despite the brevity of his stay managed to take many excellent photographs. He marvelled at the ability of one Pima band, the Quahatika, to survive in the arid desert: "A stranger would regard their sandy waste as beyond human subjection, yet these people manage to wrest an existence from it."[15]

Most of Curtis's time among the River Yumans was spent with the Mohave. He admired their physical prowess, but was less impressed by their culture and, to him, their intransigent, personalities. His work with the Upland Yumans was brief. A photograph of his camp in the snow in Walapai country symbolizes the difficulties he encountered in carrying out his task in the rugged country of the Southwest.

HOPI ON THE HOUSETOP

AT THE MEETING PLACE

CANYON DE CHELLY (NAVAHO)

SAGUARO FRUIT GATHERERS (MARICOPA)

PIMA BURDEN BEARER

CURTIS'S CAMP (WALAPAI)

SINGING TO THE SNAKES (HOPI)

A SNAKE PRIEST

ANTONIO AZUL (PIMA)

APACHE BATHING POOL

JICARILLA GIRL (APACHE)

[66]

PAPAGO WOMAN

MOHAVE MOTHER

HASCHOGAN (NAVAHO)

WALAPAI WINTER CAMP

A HOPI MAN

APACHE STORY TELLING

THE VANISHING RACE (NAVAHO)

THE PLATEAU

THE PLATEAU area includes the Columbia River Basin drainage: present day Washington and northern Oregon east of the Cascade Range, parts of British Columbia and the mountains of northern Idaho and western Montana. The area was occupied by a large number of tribes and tribelets. In the eastern mountains section were the Nez Percé, the Flathead, Pend D'Oreilles and Kutenai who were oriented toward the Plains and the buffalo that area supported, lived in skin tipis and had many horses. The Flathead are noted for their request that Catholic missionaries be sent among them, which ultimately resulted in Father Pierre-Jean De Smet's mission to them in the 1840's. The Nez Percé are noted for their valiant resistance to White encroachment on their lands, led by Chief Joseph who became a legend in his lifetime.

Further west along the Columbia River and its tributaries there were many small villages. These groups had little sense of political cohesion; 'tribal' names are used only for convenience rather than denoting a political entity, in, for example, the Yakima, the Spokan and the Okanagon groups. Some of these groups had horses and occasionally joined the Nez Percé and others in buffalo hunts on the Plains. But they were primarily oriented to the Columbia River with its abundant fish resources. They usually lived in mat houses and subsisted on salmon and other fish, berries, roots and deer.

Further down the Columbia, from the Dalles to the Pacific Ocean, were the Chinookan tribes who lived in permanent villages of cedar-board houses and subsisted principally on salmon.

The Chinookan peoples placed much emphasis on dignity, social status and material wealth. They held slaves who were usually well treated. They were great traders, acting as middlemen between tribes to the north and the south of the Columbia.

Many of the Chinook tribes disappeared by the middle of the 19th century, victims of warfare, introduced diseases and whiskey. Curtis studied one of the few remaining Chinook villages at the Dalles. He was little impressed with the people, writing, "Fish, especially salmon, were plentiful far beyond their needs and were so easily taken that the people were indolent and inert, lacking the initiative, the energetic force, the manliness characteristic of tribes whose livelihood must be gained by hunting. . . . The tribal life was one of indolent, licentious ease, . . . and filth."[16]

Many other tribes besides the Chinook had disappeared or had few surviving members. Curtis was able to photograph a Nespilim man and a Cayuse woman but could learn little about their tribes excepting the information contained in historical literature. In fact, most of Curtis's volume on the Plateau tribes is devoted to accounts of historical relations between the Indians and the Whites, especially the Yakima and Nez Percé. Curtis was a great admirer of the Nez Percé Chief Joseph and attempted to learn from him all he could about the Nez Percé's view of their struggle against White domination. Curtis's photograph of Joseph aptly portrays the integrity and strength of character of the man. In him we see a symbol of the proud heritage which Curtis labored so long to document.

WITH HER PROUDLY DECKED HORSE (CAYUSE)

WIFE OF MNAINAK (YAKIMA)

NESPILIM MAN (SALISHAM)

CHINOOK WOMAN

NEZ PERCÉ SWEAT LODGE

FLATHEAD CAMP ON A STORMY DAY

ON THE KLICKITAT RIVER

FLATHEAD BABY CARRIER

YOUNG KUTENAI GIRL

YAKIMA HOLIDAY LODGE

CHIEF JOSEPH (NEZ PERCÉ)

THE DESERT WEST

CURTIS DEVOTED a volume to the Indians of southern California and southern and western Nevada, principally the Luiseños, Cahuilla, Diegeños, Mono, Paviotso, Washo and Chemehuevi. The areas occupied by these tribes included the barren playas of the Mohave Desert and Death Valley, the desert lakes and mountains of the western Great Basin and the forested slopes of the eastern Sierra Nevadas around Lake Tahoe.

The Paviotso, a group of Northern Paiute, lived around Pyramid and Walker lakes and the Carson Sink area of western Nevada and the adjacent Honey Lake region of northeastern California. They were hunters, fishers and foragers, subsisting on seeds, roots, pinyon nut, fish, fowl, small game and sometimes insects. They lived in small family bands in temporary brush shelters or tule-mat houses, moving from place to place within their territory as various resources matured in the course of the year.

The Washo, who were neighbors of the Paviotso, followed a similar life style of hunting and foraging in the valleys at the foot of the Sierras and around Lake Tahoe. The Mono were Northern Paiute whose territory centered around Mono Lake in eastern California. Their way of life was much like that of their Paviotso relatives to the north.

The Chemehuevi were a branch of the Southern Paiute who occupied southwestern Nevada and adjacent regions of California including the heart of the barren Mohave Desert. To the southwest were the Diegeños, Luiseños and Cupeños. To the west were the Cahuilla, whose territory centered on Palm Canyon, now better known as Palm Springs.

Chemehuevi and Cahuilla territory included some of the most arid country in the United States. The population was thinly scattered over these barren tracts. The people foraged for available desert resources, moving in small family bands from place to place throughout the year. Their material culture was simple but well adapted to the harsh environment.

The Luiseños lived in a somewhat better area ecologically and were able to exploit acorn resources and, along the Pacific Coast, marine resources.

In contrast to the simple material cultures of these tribes, their mental cultures were well developed. They had a rich cosmology, and myth and ritual had a central place in their lives, especially in ceremonies centering on rites of passage. Among some tribes the *Datura* or jimson weed was given to boys as a part of their initiation into manhood. The drug induced a narcosis of up to four days' duration during which time the boys experienced visions of various supernatural animals. A particular animal became the lifelong 'Guardian Spirit' for an individual. Other American Indian tribes sought similar visions but few of them used the dangerous *Datura* as a means to that end. Boys and young men also had to endure the ordeal of being laid over red ant hills, or being placed in a hole into which the ants were poured. The ant stings were intense and the ordeal was a severe test for the youths.

By Curtis's day most Indians of the Desert West were on reservations and many of the old ways were rapidly passing away. His work with these tribes is an important early source of information about them. His photographs dramatically depict the severe environment in which they lived.

KYELLO (SANTO DOMINGO)

FRANCISCA CHIWIWI (ISLETA)

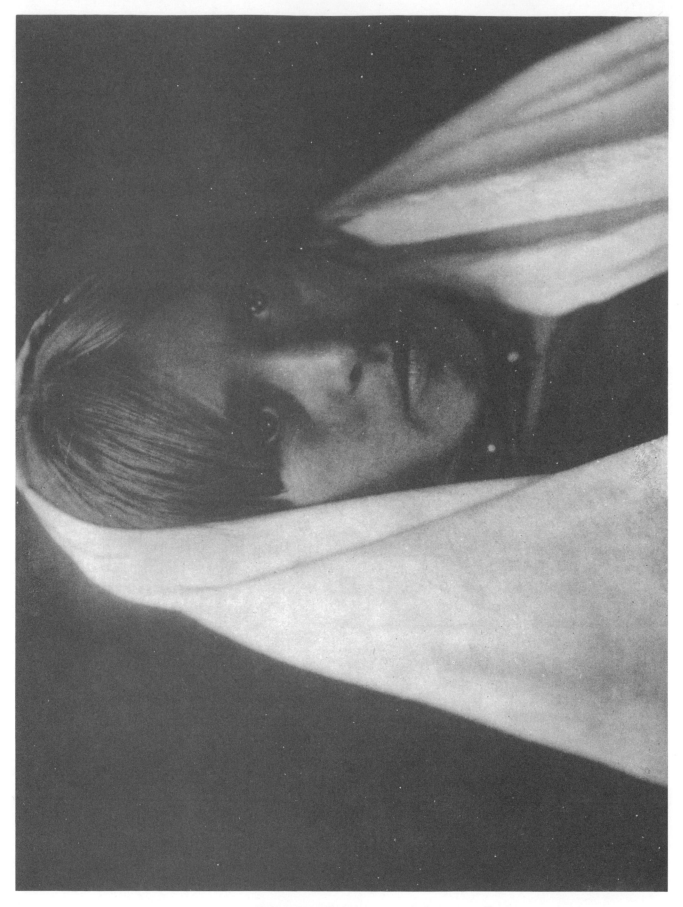

MEDICINE ROOT, TAOS

PAGUATE

A ZUNI GOVERNOR

DIEQUEÑO COMMUNAL CEREMONIAL SHELTER AT CAPITAN GRANDE

PALM CANYON

CHEMEHUEVI HOUSE

[95]

THRESHING WHEAT, TAOS

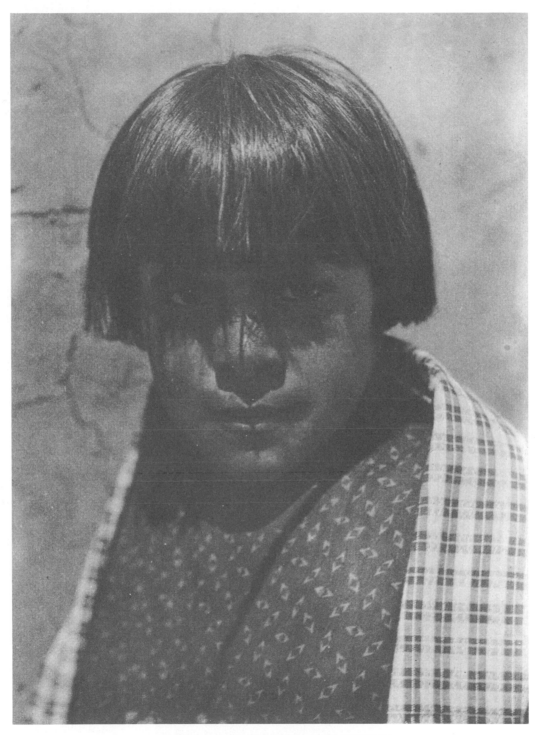

CORNSTALK (SANTO DOMINGO)

MODERN CUPEÑO HOUSE

CHEMEHUEVI HOME IN THE MESQUITE

A SOUTHERN DIEQUEÑO

MARCOS IN PALM CANYON (CAHVILLA)

A FEAST DAY AT ACOMA

THE TERRACED HOUSES OF ZUNI

A ZUNI GIRL

AMBROSIO MARTÍNEZ (PUEBLO)

NORTHERN AND CENTRAL CALIFORNIA AREA

T HE INDIANS of California present a varied picture to the anthropologist and historian. Prior to White settlement California was occupied by numerous small tribes and tribelets. California Indian cultures can be divided into three areas: northern and central California and the southern California desert, which has been treated in the Desert West section.

The Indians of northern and central California lived in small hamlets and villages. Those along the coast, especially in northwestern California and southwestern Oregon, the Hupa, Yurok, Karok, Tolowa and Tutenai, subsisted on resources of the sea, the rivers and the forest. The rich salmon and trout resources of the Klamath River and its tributaries provided an abundant food supply. Acorns, deer, roots and berries provided other resources. The people lived in plank houses and also built and used plank sweat houses and dance houses. They were expert woodworkers and basketmakers. They were very much concerned with wealth in the form of strings of dentalium shells received in trade from Indians to the north. A man's prestige and social rank depended on wealth. Marriage depended on the proper exchange of wealth and goods between families of the bride and groom. To marry without this exchange was only a 'half-marriage' and was considered socially degrading. Wealth also governed other interpersonal relations. Social relations were closely governed by elaborate unwritten codes of law. Infringing on another's rights meant that the injured party could impose a fine to settle the matter. As a result, men became experts in casuistry. Wrongs were corrected by property settlements between the individuals involved. There was no concept of a political community through which to sanction wrongs. There were aggregates of families living in villages, but no sense of community, of clan, of government or chiefs in the usual sense of those terms.

These Indians were also unique in having women shamans or curers. Such persons could heal the sick, but they might also cause sickness through sorcery and hence were often feared and treated with caution.

Further to the north and inland were the Klamath who lived in the plateau country of central and southern Oregon—in the marsh and lake area around the headwaters of the Klamath River. The Klamath were a tribe only in the linguistic sense, not by virtue of an integrated political system. They lived in small hamlets of semi-subterranean earth lodges. Like the Indians of northwestern California, the Klamath emphasized material wealth and individual achievement. Unlike the northwestern California tribes the Klamath placed much emphasis on warfare and the taking of scalps and booty. They had a rich mythology.

Curtis studied these several tribes in 1916–17. He was much taken by their cultures and regalia, took numerous photographs and devoted considerable time to collecting myths and tales.

South of the Yurok, Klamath and others in the coast ranges and the central valley of California were numerous other small Indian groups, including the Wailaki, Yuki, Pomo, Wintun, Maidu, Miwok and Yokuts. These groups subsisted on acorns, fish, nuts, berries and deer. The Pomo, for example, occupied the Russian River Valley, the adjacent coast and the Clear Lake basin between the Coast ranges. The people lived in plank or mat houses in settled villages. Unlike their northern neighbors most of these groups had definite political organizations with chiefs, often hereditary. Most groups had well-developed systems of myth and ceremony. Shamans were important but seemingly less so than to the north. Some groups, notably the Pomo, made excellent baskets, perhaps the finest in North America. Many of their feather-decorated baskets are now highly prized museum pieces.

Most of the northern and central California tribes were shattered by the White settlement of the area in the 1800's. They lacked political cohesion and a well developed tradition of warfare and hence were ill prepared to resist the massive White invasions into the gold fields and fertile valleys within their territories. By Curtis's time, many tribes had disappeared. Remnants of others were huddled on reservations or lived on the edges of towns and cities, clinging as best they could to the old ways. Curtis, and others such as A. L. Kroeber, recorded what they could. But, as in the Plains, it was all largely in the past.

LAKE POMO FISHING CAMP

IN THE FOREST (KLAMATH)

SHATILA (POMO)

A COAST POMO WOMAN

ENTRANCE TO A YUROK SWEAT HOUSE

SHERWOOD VALLEY POMO WOMAN

MAN WEARING TOLOWA DANCING HEADDRESS

LAKE POMO HUNTER

A MIXED-BLOOD COAST POMO

HUPA SWEAT HOUSE

SAM EWING (YUROK)

PRINCIPAL FEMALE SHAMAN OF THE HUPA

HUPA TROUT TRAP

NORTHWEST COAST

THE NORTHWEST coast area extends from Trinidad Bay in northern California to Yakutat Bay in southeast Alaska. Within this region anthropologists distinguish four sub-areas. One, the northwest California area, including the Yurok and Karok, is discussed under northern and central California region. The second area comprises the tribes along the coast of Oregon and Washington and the Coast Salish peoples around Puget Sound. A third area, centering on Vancouver Island and coast of British Columbia northeast of the island, includes the several Kwakiutl tribes, the Nootka, the Bella Coola and the Makah on the tip of Olympic Peninsula. The northernmost province is that of Tlingit, Haida and Tsimshian tribes occupying the Queen Charlotte Islands, Prince of Wales Island and adjacent islands and coastal areas of southeastern Alaska and British Columbia.

The cultures of the Northwest Coast were highly distinctive. The rich marine resources of the area—salmon, olachen, herring, mollusks and sea mammals provided an excellent subsistence base.

The people lived in villages set along beaches or streams. Housing styles varied but consisted of gabled, flat or shed-roofed plank structures often of considerable size. Most houses sheltered several related families.

Several characteristics of Northwest Coast society and culture stand out: highly structured social systems based on wealth with positions in the systems validated by the ceremonial distribution of great quantities of material goods in the famed potlatches; well developed mythology and related ceremonial and dancing complexes. Among some groups, such as the Kwakiutl, myth cycles and associated ceremonies were very elaborate, with masked dancers representing mythical beings, and the use of legerdemain and wooden puppets involved in the performances. Another unique feature was the distinctive art of the area, especially wood carving. Wood carving was highly developed in ornamenting utilitarian items, such as storage boxes, canoe prows, utensils, as well as in the so-called 'totem' poles carved by groups in the more northerly areas.

Not all groups within the area had cultures elaborated to the same degree. Social ranking was most important in the Kwakiutl areas and to the north, although other groups had such distinctions.

Curtis had begun his study of Indians among the Coast Salish groups around Puget Sound. As noted in the Introduction to this volume, his earliest Indian photographs were of these people, such as the picture of "Princess Angeline," daughter of Chief Siahl, after whom Seattle was named. He ultimately devoted three of his twenty volumes to the Indians of the Northwest Coast including one whole volume, with more pages than any other, on the Kwakiutl.

Many of the tribes along the Oregon Seaboard and around Puget Sound were extinct, or nearly so, by 1900. As Curtis wrote about the Puget Sound tribes, "Some . . . still exist; others, extinct, have left a memento of themselves in geographic names; some are known only as names recorded by an early traveler or remembered by an aged survivor of the native population."[17] Such groups include the Squaxon, Sahewamish, Suquamish, Snohomish and Stillaquamish.

But other groups were still functioning, although their populations had severely declined. Curtis spent parts of several years studying the Quinault, Quilliute, Makah, and the Nootka of Vancouver Island who were all whalers, hunting the large sea mammals on the open sea in canoes with harpoons, the only Northwest Indians to do so. He briefly visited the Haida of Queen Charlotte Islands. But his major effort was to study the Kwakiutl.

Although Northwest Coast culture had severely declined by the early 1900's, Curtis was able to capture much of its flavor in his photographs — the emphasis on social status, the dependence on the rich marine resources of the area, and the highly elaborate and unique art and ceremonialism.

A KOEKSOTENOK HOUSE FRONT

A NAKOAKTOK CHIEF'S DAUGHTER

A MAMALELEKALA CHIEF'S MORTUARY HOUSE

A KOSKIMO HOUSE-POST

COWICHAN SPEARING SALMON

NEAH BAY VILLAGE

SNOHOMISH GRAVE HOUSE

QUILCENE BOY (TWANA)

[129]

THE MOUTH OF QUINAULT RIVER

KWAKIUTL HOUSE-FRAME

DIGGING SKUNK CABBAGE ROOTS (SALISHAM)

PRINCESS ANGELINE (SUGUAMISH)

WHALING FLOATS (NOOTKA)

MAKAH WHALER

RETURN OF THE HALIBUT FISHERS

A BRIDAL GROUP

COWICHAN MASKED DANCER

THE ESKIMO

THE ESKIMO peoples occupy an enormous area of the Arctic regions of North America, the eastern tip of Siberia and the east and west coasts of Greenland. In Alaska the Eskimos occupy the coast and adjacent interior regions from Prince William Sound in southeastern Alaska, around the perimeter of the state (including the Aleutian Islands) to the Canadian border in the north. Several sub-groups of Alaskan Eskimos can be distinguished. The South Alaskan Eskimo center on the Kenai and Alaskan peninsulas; the Aleut occupy the Aleutian Islands; the West Alaskan Eskimo territory centers on Nunivak Island and Norton Sound; the Bering Strait Eskimo center on the Seward Peninsula and around Kotzebue Sound; and the North Alaskan Eskimo occupy the coast and adjacent interior regions from Point Barrow to Mackenzie Bay in extreme northwestern Canada.

Throughout the entire area from Greenland to southern Alaska there is a remarkable uniformity in physical type, culture and language of the Eskimo. They form a distinctive physical sub-group of the Mongoloid racial stock. Although differing in details, Eskimo culture is closely adapted to the tundra and the sea and the harsh Arctic climate. Subsistence is based on marine resources, fish, seals, walruses and whales, and tundra-dwelling animals including the caribou or American reindeer. Polar bears are also hunted where they occur. Eskimos from Greenland to Alaska speak a series of closely related, mutually intelligible languages.

Edward Curtis first saw the South Alaskan Eskimo in 1899 when he was with the Harriman Expedition. In the summer of 1927 he returned to Alaska to study and photograph the Eskimo of western Alaska from the Aleutian Islands to Point Barrow, concentrating on the people from Nunivak Island to the north shore of Kotzebue Sound, that is, the West Alaskan and Bering Strait groups. He found the people still pursuing a traditional way of life, "exceptionally happy because they have been little affected by contact with civilization."[18] Clusters of wooden, earth-covered houses were scattered along terraces overlooking the sea. (Only the Central Eskimo of Canada build snow igloos.) The houses were occupied by small independent families, basic political units, there being no concept of a larger political organization. The people subsisted on the resources of the sea. Whales were pursued and harpooned by small crews of men in open boats, called umiaks. Seals and walruses were hunted by individual men in covered kayaks, or stalked on ice floes. Fish were taken from the sea and the rivers by a variety of techniques. The people wore tailored skin clothing, actually two suits of skins with the fur inward, providing an insulating air layer between.

Curtis's brief stay afforded him an opportunity to study only the summer activities of the people. As elsewhere, however, he collected myths and tales and all the details he could of daily life. He saw the Eskimo at a time when they still pursued much of their traditional way of life. White civilization was encroaching—e.g., guns were replacing spears and bows and arrows—but the culture had not been overwhelmed as had others which Curtis knew. The old ways were still a living reality for the Eskimo, and not simply memories growing dim in the minds of the aged.

NUNIVAK KAYAK FRAME

HOOPER BAY HOMES

NUNIVAK FISH-DRYING RACKS

KING ISLAND VILLAGE (ESKIMO)

NOATAK KAYAKS

LAUNCHING THE WHALE BOAT (ESKIMO)

NOATAK FAMILY GROUP

NUNIVAK CHILDREN

NOTES

1. Edward S. Curtis, *The North American Indian,* 20 vols. (Cambridge University Press, 1907–30), vol. III, p. 49.
2. *op. cit.,* vol. I, p. *xiii.*
3. *ibid.*
4. *ibid.,* p. *xiv.*
5. *ibid.,* pp. *xvi–xvii.*
6. *op. cit.,* vol. XII, p. 4.
7. *op. cit.,* vol. X, p. 4.
8. *op. cit.,* vol. II, p. *xi.*
9. *op. cit.,* vol. XX, folio, picture caption no. 688.
10. George B. Grinnell, "Portraits of Indian Types," *Scribner's Magazine,* XXXVII, pp. 272–73 (1905).
11. Curtis, *op. cit.,* vol. III, p. *xi.*
12. *op. cit.,* vol. I, p. *xx.*
13. *ibid.,* p. 79.
14. *ibid.,* p. 80.
15. *op. cit.,* vol. II, p. *xii.*
16. *op. cit.,* vol. VIII, pp. 85, 87.
17. *op. cit.,* vol. IX, p. 14.
18. *op. cit.,* vol. XX, folio, picture caption no. 688.

BIBLIOGRAPHICAL NOTES

THE ORIGINAL edition of Curtis's *North American Indians* (Cambridge, 1907–1930) was limited to five hundred sets, priced at $5,000 a set, and is now to be found only in major libraries. The set has recently (1970) been reprinted by Johnson Reprint Corporation of New York. The primary biographical source on Curtis is Ralph W. Andrews, *Curtis' Western Indians* (New York, 1962). The reports of the Harriman expedition contain many Curtis photographs: C. Hart Merriam (ed.), *Harriman Alaska Series*, 14 vols., published by the Smithsonian Institution (Washington, 1890–1910). Curtis published several illustrated articles and two books on various Indian tribes between 1906 and 1915: "Vanishing Indian Types—The Tribes of the Southwest," *Scribner's Magazine*, XXXIX, pp. 513–29 (1906); "Vanishing Indian Types—The Tribes of the Northwest Plains," *Scribner's Magazine*, XXXIX, pp. 657–71 (1906); "Indians of the Stone Houses," *Scribner's Magazine*, XLV, pp. 161–75 (1909); "Village Tribes of the Desert Land," *Scribner's Magazine*, XLV, pp. 275–87 (1909); *Indian Days of Long Ago* (New York, 1914); *Land of the Head Hunters* (New York, 1915). Articles about Curtis's work include: George Bird Grinnell, "Portraits of Indian Types," *Scribner's Magazine*, XXXVII, pp. 258–73 (1905); Anonymous, "A Record of the Indians," *The World's Work*, XII, pp. 7913–14 (1906); "Telling History by Photographs: Records of Our North American Indians Being Preserved by Pictures," *Craftsman*, IX, pp. 846–49 (1906); Edmond S. Meany, "Hunting Indians with a Camera," *The World's Work*, XV, pp. 10004–11 (1908).

There is an abundance of primary sources on North American Indians. The major bibliographic source available in many libraries is George Peter Murdock, *Ethnographic Bibliography of North America*, 3rd edition (New Haven, 1960). Standard general sources include: Frederick Webb Hodge (ed.), "Handbook of American Indians North of Mexico," 2 vols., *Bureau of American Ethnology Bulletin* no. 30 (Washington, 1907–10; reprinted, New York, 1960); Edward H. Spicer, *A Short History of the Indians of the United States*, (New York, 1969); John R. Swanton, "The Indian Tribes of North America," *Bureau of American Ethnology Bulletin* no. 145 (Washington, 1952); Robert F. Spencer, Jesse D. Jennings *et. al.*, *The Native Americans* (New York, 1965); Clark Wissler, *The American Indian* (New York, 1938); Ruth Underhill, *Red Man's America* (Chicago, 1946); John Collier, *Indians of the Americas* (New York, 1947); Harold E. Driver, *Indians of North America* (Chicago, 1961).

Works on the Indians of specific areas include Robert F. Spencer, "The North Alaskan Eskimo," *Bureau of American Ethnology Bulletin* no. 171 (Washington, 1959); Philip Drucker, *Indians of the Northwest Coast* (New York, 1955, reprinted 1963); Robert H. Lowie, *Indians of the Plains* (New York, 1954, reprinted 1963); A. L. Kroeber, "Handbook of the Indians of California," *Bureau of American Ethnology Bulletin* no. 78 (Washington, 1925); Edward P. Dozier, *The Pueblo Indians of North America* (New York, 1970); Homer G. Barnett, *The Coast Salish of British Columbia* (Eugene, [Ore.], 1955); K. Birket-Smith, *The Eskimos*, 2nd ed. (New York, 1958); E. F. Castetter and W. H. Bell, *Pima and Papago Indian Agriculture* (Albuquerque, 1942); and *Yuman Indian Agriculture* (Albuquerque, 1951); D. Jenness, *The Indians of Canada*, 3rd ed., *Bulletin of the Canadian National Museum* no. 65 (Ottawa, 1955); A. Joseph, R. Spicer and J. Chesky, *The Desert People* (Chicago, 1949); C. Kluckhohn and D. Leighton, *The Navaho* (Cambridge, 1946, reprinted New York, 1960); Verne F. Ray, *Cultural Relations in the Plateau of Northwestern America* (Los Angeles, 1939); and F. G. Roe, *The Indian and the Horse* (Norman, [Okla.], 1955).

LIST OF ILLUSTRATIONS AND SOURCE REFERENCES